AMAZON ECHO SHOW 8 USERS GUIDE

The Complete User Manual for Beginners and Pro to Master the New Amazon Echo Show 8 with Tips & Tricks for Alexa Skills

Aaron Madison

Table of Contents

Introduction

The Amazon Echo Show 8 now has an improved smart speaker that is perfect for home control and a quality sound for music, video, games, podcasts, phone calls, broadcasting, and lots more. The device is available in four color variants, namely, charcoal, twilight blue, heather gray, and sandstone. This book will teach you how to set up and use the essential features of the new Amazon Echo 8. If you ever wanted to learn every important and feature of your Echo device, then you found the right guide. This guide will help you optimize your Amazon Echo, boost productivity and efficiency and maximize your Echo's full potential; this manual provides proven and tested step by step instructions to help you use your Echo device better than a Pro. The images and illustrations are comprehensive enough to guide and help you find solutions to all features of your Amazon Echo and to troubleshoot common problems swiftly. Happy reading!

Preview of Echo Show 8

In 2018 Amazon rebranded the main 10-inch Echo Show (2nd gen) and early 2019 it launched the Echo Show 5. Again the company have released another model called the Echo Show 8. However, the Show 8 is more like a bigger Show 5 rather than a smaller Echo Show. Reason been that the standard Echo Show has over-large bezels and a very largish design. There's a privacy shutter on top, as with other Amazon Echo devices you can use the mute button to disable the camera and microphone. The gadget is available in white or black.

The display of the Echo Show 8 is much better than the Echo Show 2nd generation. The sound quality of the Show 8 is better than the Show 5. The Echo Show 8 has dual 2-inch speakers with passive bass.

As usual Amazon's own Android fork - Fire OS is used to power the device. The gadget works fine, especially for basic commands such as checking the traffic, weather, alarm or pulling up your calendar, and also Alexa skills.

Technical Specifications:

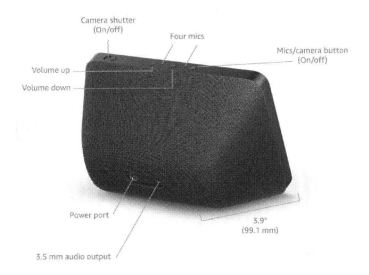

Size: 7.9"x 5.4"x 3.9"

Screen: 8.0" touch screen

Screen resolution: (1280 x 800p)

Speakers: 2 x 2.0" @ 10W per channel

Camera: 1MP with built-in camera shutter along with microphone/camera off button

Weight: 1037 grams

Wi-Fi connectivity: Dual-band Wi-Fi supports 802.11a/b/g/n/ac Wi-Fi networks. Does not connect to peer-to-peer Wi-Fi networks.

Audio: 2.0" (52 mm) neodymium speakers

Processor: MediaTek MT 8163

Alexa App: Alexa App is supported on Fire OS, Android, and iOS devices.

3

Content in the box: Amazon Echo Show 8, power adapter (30W)/cable and a quick start guide.

Bluetooth connection: The Advanced Audio Distribution Profile (A2DP) is supported to stream audio from mobile devices to Echo Show 8 or from the Echo Show 8 to Bluetooth speakers. Audio/Video Remote Control Profile (AVRCP) for voice control of connected mobile devices. Hands-free voice control is not compatible with Mac OS X devices. Bluetooth speakers that require a PIN code are not compatible.

CHAPTER 1- Setting up Echo Show 8

Set Up Echo Show 8

- Download the Alexa App to your mobile device (iOS 9.0 or higher, Android 5.0 or higher, FireOS 3.0 or higher). The app can be downloaded from the Amazon Appstore, Apple App Store, or Google Play. You can likewise download the app from alexa.amazon.com.
- After downloading the Alexa app, place your Echo Show eight inches or more from dividers or windows and fit it into an AC power outlet utilizing the power adapter. Your device will turn on automatically.
- Once on, you would hear Alexa say, **"Hello, your Echo Device is ready for setup."**
- Next, unpack your Amazon Echo Show, and plug the power connector into the device and after that into a wall outlet.
- Allow the Echo Show to boot up and load up its initialization process.
- When the initialization procedure is done, select your language, and connect the Echo Show to your home Wi-Fi network.
- When connected to a Wi-Fi network, select your current time zone, and sign in to your Amazon account.

- Acknowledge the Echo Show Terms and Conditions, and let your Echo Show update its firmware.
- Once the firmware is updated, you're cool to start enjoying your Echo Show and have unchartered access to Amazon Prime Video, music streaming, stream recipes, and many more.

Pair Mobile Device with Echo Show

- Place your mobile device to Bluetooth pairing mode.
- Ensure the mobile device is in range of your Echo.
- Say, "**Pair,**" Alexa tells you that Echo is prepared to combine. To exit Bluetooth pairing mode, say, "**Cancel**."
- Launch the Bluetooth settings menu on your smartphone, and select your Echo. Alexa lets you know whether the connection is successful or not.
- To pair, later on, you can say, "**Connect**." If connected with other devices, your Echo connects with the most recent paired device.
- To unpair your device from the Echo Show. Just say, "**Disconnect**."

Set Up Alexa Voice Profiles

Having multiple individuals in your household, utilizing a similar profile on all the Echo devices in your home, can be somewhat confounding, particularly since everybody has various needs and needs from the Alexa smart assistant. Amazon has a response for that with Alexa Voice Profiles.

Follow the process below to set up your voice profile quickly.

- Say "**Alexa, Learn My Voice**," once your Echo has been setup.
- Alexa will ask you about your identity in your Amazon profile. Reply with "**No**" until your name is reached; at that point, reply with "**Yes.**"
- Recite the phrases that Alexa requests that you repeat.
- After completion, Alexa will have learned in your voice!

You can likewise set up Alexa Voice Profiles utilizing the Alexa App for Android by following the steps below:

- Open the Alexa app.
- Log in to the Amazon account that is connected with all the Echo devices in your household.
- Tap the **Menu** symbol in the upper left corner of your screen.
- Select **Settings**.

- Choose **Alexa Account**.
- Tap **Recognized Voices**.

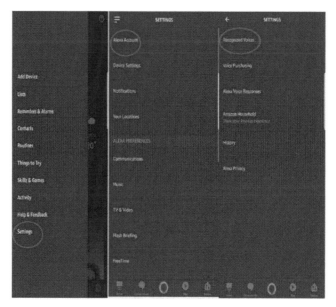

- Click **Your Voice**.
- Once on this screen, you'll be welcome to make your first voice profile. Tap **Begin**.

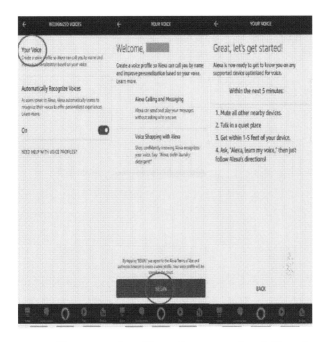

- Adhere to the directions on the following screen in 5 minutes.
- Whenever completed, your voice profile will be set up.

Delete Your Alexa Voice Profile

- Tap on the **Menu icon** (3-dash lines) and select **Settings**
- From the display options, tap **Alexa Account**, then select **Recognized Voices**
- Next, select **Your Voice**
- Tap "**Delete my voice.**"

9

Help Alexa Recognize Voice

The **Your Voice** menu in the Alexa app offers an option to help Alexa recognize different voices.

- To go through another training session with Alexa tap **"Learn my voice"** from the **Your Voice** menu if you want to go through another training session with Alexa. For training to quickly help Alexa master your voice, you can play more recorded phrases from another household member with a voice profile.

- You then tap the name of the person who uttered the phrase so Alexa can more easily identify each speaker. To set this up, tap **"Get started."**

- At the next screen, tap **Begin**. Play their first phrase and then select the name of the speaker. Continue with each screen until you hit the final lane of set up, then tap **Finish**.

Listen to More Phrases

At the **"Great job!"** display screen, click **"Listen to More Phrases"** for more voice training. Alexa will then take you through another round of recordings if you feel Alexa has gotten the hang of the voices in your household, exit the training.

Set up Amazon Household

With an Amazon Household, you and other individuals from the family can share the advantages of an Amazon Prime account alongside access to Kindle eBooks and numerous digital content from Amazon using Echo devices.

In the Alexa app, you can include a maximum of two adults. However, you can't include kids from the Household Profile setting; that requires a different procedure through Amazon FreeTime; with this, you can add up to four youngster accounts. Here are the procedures to do that.

- To start with, open the Alexa app on your smartphone or tablet and ensure you're logged in with your Amazon account. Tap on the menu icon (☰) in the upper-left corner and afterward tap **Settings > Alexa Account > Amazon Household**. From here, you're ready to invite a household member.

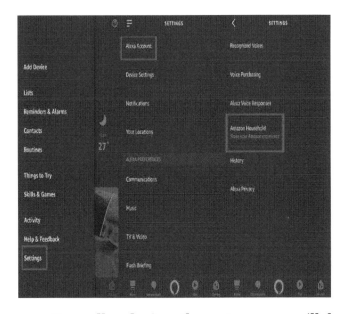

- Secondly, during the setup, you will be required to input the individual's Amazon username and password. Ask the grownup you need to add to type their Amazon username and password. Next, tap the **Verify Account** button. (If the individual doesn't have an Amazon account, they will have the alternative to make one.)

Amazon Households

The invited adult should enter their account information to join the household.

Forgot password?

Show password

Keep me signed in. Details

Verify Account

- When the individual's account data has been included, you would then notice a screen inviting them to Amazon Households. Tap the "**Join household**" link to add the individual. The following screen discloses to you that the Household has been made and that you and the new individual are members of the Amazon Household. The screen additionally offers a couple of brisk tips for utilizing Alexa in a household.

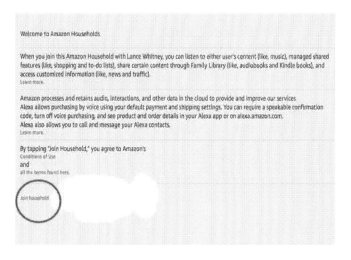

- Lastly, the individual needs to sign in to the Alexa app on a device to finish the procedure. If they intend to utilize a similar device as you, log out of the app and have them log back in with their very own account details. At the Setup screen, have the new individual tap on their name. They would then be able to experience the various screens to view and work with different Alexa skills and requests.

Add a Child Account to Household

- You should initially set up FreeTime to add a child to your Alexa-empowered device. Set this up in the Alexa app by tapping **Devices** at the bottom right of the screen. Next, select **Echo & Alexa** to see a rundown of your associated Echo devices, and tap the Echo you need to add the kid too.

- Under the device's settings, tap on the access to FreeTime. On the following screen, flip the button to turn on FreeTime. A screen will spring up to give details about the feature. Follow up by tapping the **Setup Amazon FreeTime** button to proceed. At the following screen, you will have the choice to deactivate certain features, tap **Continue** and watch a video, tap the "**X**" at the upper-right of the screen to close the window.

Turn Off Amazon FreeTime

- To deactivate FreeTime, you'll have to go back to the screen where you had first set up the feature and toggle off the button for FreeTime.
- The app requests affirmation. Tap the **Turn Off** button, with this FreeTime, is now disabled for that Echo while the account returns to the last adult who utilized the device.
- However, if you can't remember which account is active ask "Alexa, which account is this?" and Alexa will identify the account for you.

Local Voice Control with Offline Echo Devices

The Local Voice Control features execute requests such as controlling compatible lights, plugs, and switches when an Echo device with an integrated smart home hub is not connected to the internet.

However, after your Echo device recovers its internet connection, your requests are sent to the cloud and are accessible to review in the Alexa app. To configure the Local Voice Control setting in the Alexa app, follow the steps below:

- Select the **Devices** pictogram.
- Select **Local Voice Control,** and after that, flip the switch to turn "**On**" or "**Off**."

If your Echo with an in-built smart home hub isn't connected to the Internet, you can utilize your voice to:

- Control compatible smart home devices, including switches, lights, and attachments that are directly connected to your Echo device.
- Stop or cancel, updates, and timers and alarms that were set before your Echo device were disconnected.
- Request the time or date.
- Control the device's volume.
- Alexa additionally reacts to the request, "What quests can you complete offline?"

To check if your compatible smart home device is directly connected with your Echo device with an integrated smart home hub, go to the Alexa app:

- Select the **Devices** pictogram.
- Swipe to your smart home device.
- Select the settings symbol and after that, scan the **Connected Via** information.

CHAPTER 2- Personalizing your Echo Show, Photos & Selfies

Customize the Home Screen on Your Echo Show

To manage and customize the home screen of your Echo Show is simple. Here's how to do it:

- Swipe down from the top of the screen and tap **Settings** (the gear icon).
- Swipe downward and click **Home and Clock**.
- Choose **Clock**.
- Next, select from the rays of options; Playful, Photography, Recent Clocks, Personal, Classic, and Modern Photos.
- Irrespective of which option you select, there are multiple patterns to pick from. These clocks have a different background that will cycle by default. However, if you prefer to choose a single background, swipe to a clock and tap the **pencil icon** (edit button) at the top and tap **Background**. Look through the changed choices and click the checkmark to save.
- You can likewise alter how the outlook of the clock face. The clock faces to choose ranges from moderate analog appearances

to modern digital clocks. To select another clock face, tap the **pencil icon** (edit button) and choose **Clock Face**. Swipe to your preferred outlook and tap the checkmark.

Manage Night Mode

If you keep an Echo Show by your bedside, you likely don't need it showing information at full brightness, As opposed to manually reducing the brightness when you get in bed, you can activate Night Mode any time of the day, and it can take effect at night. Follow the steps below to do that.

- To do this, go to **Settings**
- Select **Home and Clock**
- Choose **Night Mode,** and tap **Enable Nighttime Clock**. Furthermore, underneath that, you can set a timer for when the clock face should dim and when Nighttime Clock should be activated every day.

Add Facebook Photos to Echo Home Screen

The odds of you owning a Facebook account are far more than the odds of you utilizing Amazon Photos, so we'll begin here. You can add your Facebook photos to appear on the display of your Echo Show; you can manually select or have the whole albums automatically check-marked and start showing on your Echo Show, here's how to do this:

- Launch the Alexa app on your phone.
- Select the **menu button (Ξ)**
- Tap **Settings**.
- Swipe down to **Photos** and under **Facebook**, tap **Link account**.
- You'll be redirected to a page where you'll have to sign in to your Facebook account and authorize Alexa to get access to your photos.

That's not the end, to make the photos appear on the screen of your Echo Show, the steps are crucial:

- Swipe down from the top of the screen on your Echo Show and choose **Settings**.
- Choose **Home & Clock**
- At that point, tap **Clock**.
- Click on **Personal Photos**.
- Choose **Background**.
- Select the Facebook option and then select the albums you want to connect to Alexa.
- Follow up by tapping the **Save** button at the base of the screen, and you're through with the process. Your Echo device will begin to show your Facebook photos on the background of your Echo Show.
- You can likewise have Alexa show your photos in a by saying, "Alexa, show my

photos" or "Alexa, show my photo collections."

Add Amazon Photos on Echo Show Home Screen

If you have access to Amazon Photo service, you can make your photos appear on your Echo Show background by following the steps below:

- Go to the Amazon Photos site and ensure logged in to the same account linked to your Echo device.
- Next, tap **Albums**
- Select **Create album**.
- Drag and drop the photo you want into the collection, save and then name the album.
- Next, swipe down from the top of your Echo Show tap **Settings**.
- Choose **Home and Clock**
- At that point, click on **Clock**.
- Choose **Personal Photos** and tap on **Background**.
- Tap the **Amazon Photos** option.
- At that point, select the album(s) you want to connect with Alexa.
- Finish by tapping **Save** at the bottom of the display.
- Once more, saying "Alexa, show my photos" or "Alexa, show my photo

collections" will put your photos on display. You can likewise request Alexa to display specific collections by saying the exact name of the album.

Take Selfies on Echo Show

This is one of the simplest questions you'll ever ask Alexa, and guess what? It's straightforward to take a selfie on your Echo Show say, "Alexa, take my picture." Next, different camera choices will pop up, and you'll be prompted to choose a camera type before the image is taken.

At the point when Alexa requests that you pick a camera, pick one of the three choices displayed. Say the name of the camera or simply the number.

A five-second timer will start. Once the five-seconds count elapses, Alexa will snap your image. All Photo Booth pictures will directly be sent to your Amazon Photos library.

Viewing your photos on the Echo Show

To view your photos, say, "Alexa, show me my photo collections." Alexa will then show all of your Prime Photos collections. You would then be able to choose the ones you want to view from the Photo Booth collection.

Delete Photos on the Echo Show

- Open the Prime Photos app on your mobile device.
- Click on **Albums** at the bottom of the display.
- Select **Photo Booth**.
- Select the photograph you wish to delete and then click on the three vertical dot
- Tap **Delete**.
- Select **Move to Trash** to confirm the deletion.

Setup Minimal Home Screen Backgrounds

If you prefer your Echo device not to display any photo apart from the usual standard illustrations, you can quickly do that by following the steps below:

- Go to **Settings**
- Choose **Display**
- Tap **Theme** and select **Minimal**. That does the job for you!

CHAPTER 3- - Routines, Blueprints & More

Set up Routines

Routines can gather complex commands and multi-step tasks into a straightforward command, and here's the way to benefit as much as possible. You can make Routines as straightforward or mind-boggling as you'd like, and to enable you to begin, we have a couple of tips to make the procedure as simple as anyone might imagine. To start with, we should make a Routine that is initiated by voice command:

- Launch the Alexa app and then click on the Menu icon in the upper left corner of the screen.
- Select **Routines**.
- Follow by clicking the plus icon "+" in the upper right side of the display.
- Next, tap "**When this happens**."

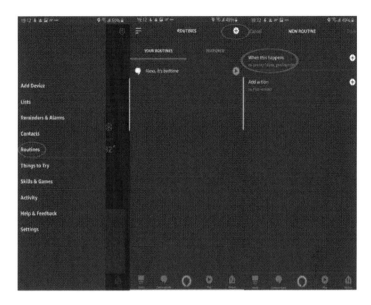

- Select **Voice**.
- Type in your trigger phrase and tap **Save**.
- Tap **Add action**

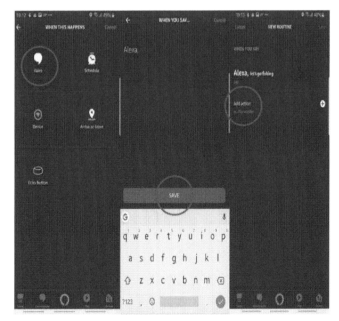

- Select the activities/actions you want to include.
- Tap **Save** in the upper right corner of the screen once you've included all your ideal actions.

Things get more interesting right here; you can customize Alexa to play music, get you up on the news, control your smart home devices, brief you on the traffic, change your Echo's volume, and inform you about the weather, welcome you, show photos and so much more. You're at leisure to include as many of these actions and command you desire; you can also rearrange their position by holding down on the six dots close to each command and moving them up or down.

Set up Scheduled Routines

If you want your routine to go on or off at a certain time during the day, the following steps will help you realize that:

- From the Alexa app, tap the menu icon in the upper left corner of the screen.
- Select **Routines**.
- Next, click on the plus icon "+" at the upper right side of the display.
- Select **When this happens**.
- Tap **Schedule**.
- Tap **At Time**.
- Select the hour you need your routine to go off.

- Choose the minute you need your routine to go off.
- Tap **OK**.
- Tap **Repeat** if you fancy the routine to go off regularly.
- Tap the days you want it to go off.
- Tap **Done**.
- Tap **Done** again.
- Tap **Add action**.
- Tap the action you wish to include, for example, music and type the song you wish to play, then choose the source from which the song will play.
- Tap **Next**.
- Tap **Save**.

You can see your Routines from the Routines page in the Alexa app, and tapping on a current one will give you controls to manage the routine.

Alexa Blueprints

From the Alexa Blueprints portal, you can make your very own skills for Alexa; this implies you can further modify Alexa exactly as you would prefer.

You can even share your customized skills, and the exciting part is that you don't need coding skills to utilize Blueprints either. You need to modify one of the templates Amazon has available. Here's the way to make your very own Alexa skill.

- Begin by going to blueprints.amazon.com. When you're there, click on the sign-in button at the top right corner of the screen and sign in with your Amazon account info.
- Next, start by choosing a blueprint. Think about the Alexa Blueprints is a collection of different templates. Search for Blueprints divided into different categories.
- After locating a Blueprint layout that you like, click on it. Doing so will display an outline of the blueprint and the steps on how to create such a blueprint. The Play button allows you to hear a sample of the blueprint before proceeding to create and modify.
- To confirm you want to create the Blueprint-building process, tap on the "**Make Your Own**" link at the top. For greeting cards, tap on **Pick a Theme**.
- The following screen you see includes various form fields. You can delete the filled space, edit the details to your taste. Next, tap the **Next** button in the upper right corner of the screen after editing the fields.
- Picking a name for your skill is one of the last strides to hover. Picking one may appear to be clear; however, you should remember Alexa's has certain limitations,

so choose a simple and straightforward name for your skill.

- Next, look out for the notification message indicating that your skill is ready for use. You can likewise go to the "**Skills You've Made**" link at the top of the screen; this section displays all the skills you've made with Alexa blueprint, if it displays that your skill is "**Ready to Use and edit**," you can feel free to launch the skill.

- You can begin using the skill by using "Alexa, open [skill name]" voice command. If the skill doesn't work as you had expected, you can modify by clicking on the "**Skills You've Made**" section.

- When you've tried your skill, and you realize it works how you need it to, you can decide to share it with family and friends on various social media outlets. To do so, go under **Skills You've Made** tab, select **Details,** and tap **Share With Others**.

- You can publish your skill to the Alexa Skills Store for Alexa users in the U.S. to discover, use, and review.

To publish your skill, it will have to go through review procedures that typically takes around a couple of business days. However, if you've shared your skill, you'll have to disavow sharing to facilitate the publishing aspect. Here are the procedures on how you can publish your Alexa skill:

- Go to **Skills You've Made** tab and click on the skill you wish to publish.
- Tap **Publish to Skills Store**
- Input your Alexa Skills Store name, which is how customers will discover you in the Alexa Skills Store. The name of your Skills Store can be is not compulsorily the name of your skill. Fill in all the details needed.
- Go to the following page and select the category your skill fits into, make sure you pick important keywords that will help individuals discover your skill and then add a short and detailed description of your skill in the appropriate field.
- On the following page, input the policy information of your skill and its target group.
- On the next page, access all info you provided and submit your skill to be looked into by Amazon for approval.
- Anticipate an email notice telling you whether your skill has been approved or disallowed.
- You may make a few skills that aren't as valuable or fun as you'd anticipate. The Skills You've Made section enables you to customize a skill. On the other hand, you can erase a skill to delete it from your account. You can likewise delete skills you've published on the Alexa Skills Store by choosing **Remove** from Store under the menu options.

Alexa Guard

The Guard is an Alexa feature that serves as surveillance and also acts as the ears of your home while you are out of the house. On the off chance that the far-field microphones in any of your Echo devices recognize something that sounds dangerous like your house is engulfed by fire or there's an attempt to burgle your home through the breaking of glass, Alexa will quickly hop and send a smart alert notification to your mobile device.

The smart alerts incorporate a ten-second audio recording of the incident, so you can affirm what the commotion was for yourself before making a judgment. It additionally has a button to access Alexa's "Drop-In" feature, enabling you to further scrutinize the incident, with your Echo Show you can drop in through video too. The steps below will help you set up this feature for your home:

- Open the Alexa app.
- Click on the **Menu** icon.
- Look down and press "**Settings**."
- Tap "**Guard**."
- Slide down and tap "**Set up Guard**."
- If you need Guard to trigger when Alexa hears a smoke alarm, breaking and shattering of glass, overflowing water tap "**Add**." Otherwise, tap "**Later**."

- You'll be given an outline of the feature you added to Guard. In case you're happy with your decisions, tap "**Confirm**."
- The Alexa app tells you when the Guard Setup is complete, from the bottom of the screen, tap "**Done**" to finalize. You might be required to permit the Alexa app to send you Smart Alerts; you'll have to allow this function for the Guard feature to work. To activate this feature when you're going out of your house, say, "Alexa, I'm leaving." When you return home, say "Alexa, I'm home" to switch Guard back to Home Mode. Alternatively, you can likewise flip between modes manually on the Alexa app.

Alexa Hunches

Hunches inform you when something might be strange with an associated smart home device. Hunches are a discretionary Alexa feature that signals you when one of your associated smart home devices isn't in its regular state. Alexa can offer a hunch after you state certain expressions, for example, "Goodnight" or "Set timer." You can likewise ask Alexa, "Do you have any hunches?"

If Alexa recognizes that an associated smart home device isn't in a state you like, Alexa tells you and offers to fix it. For instance, if you state "Goodnight," and you've neglected to switch off the lights, Alexa alarms you and offers to turn it off. To acknowledge a hunch, say, "Yes." To dismiss a hunch, say, "No." You can likewise disregard the hunch.

Alexa gives hunches to associated smart home devices, for example, plugs, lights, bolts, and switches. By default, "Hunches" is turned on. To disable, say, "Disable Hunches." To turn it on again, just say, "Enable Hunches." However, you can decide to turn on or off the feature from the Alexa app on your mobile device.

- Launch the Alexa app.
- Tap on **Menu** and select **Settings**.
- Select **Hunches**.
- Turn Hunch on or off using the toggle.

CHAPTER 4- Music, Radio, Podcasts & Audiobooks

Set Up Multi-Room Music

From the Alexa app on your mobile device, tap the Smart Home Control tab (house-shaped symbol in the bottom right corner).

- Click on the plus sign (+) in the upper right side of the screen.
- Tap "**Add Multi-Room Music Speakers**."
- You have to group your speakers for them to play the same songs. To create a group, give it a name.
- You'll then notice your Echo units that can be placed in a listed group. Select the ones you need to incorporate into this group, after which, tap "**Save**." You have to know that each speaker can only be added to one group. For example, if Speaker A is already added to Group 1, you cannot add it again to Group 2.
- To remove a speaker from a group, select the group the speaker is added to under the "**Speaker Groups**" option in the Smart Home Control tab. Next, tap "**Unpair Speaker System**."
- When the group is set up, you can play music by saying, "Play music [Echo group name]."

Listen to Music

The simplest method to listen to music on your Echo device is via a music-streaming service. It is worthy to note that your Echo will connect to Amazon Music by default. In case you're an Amazon Prime subscriber, you can catch over 2 million songs from Prime Music freely, or stream10 million songs if you upgrade to Amazon Music Unlimited. Be that as it may, you can likewise get to other prominent services and remotely stream music to your Echo device from your phone, tablet, or PC. The steps to follow and get the music rolling is well documented below;

- After you set up your Amazon Echo, you can connect other music services, such as; Amazon Music, iHeartRadio, TuneIn, Apple Music, Deezer, Spotify, Gimme, SiriusXM, Tidal, Pandora and Vevo. You'll require an account or membership with each music service before you can get to it through your Echo.
- If you need to tune in to music through your preferred streaming service, you will initially need to connect it with Alexa. Tap the menu button (Ξ) in the upper left corner and go to **Settings > Music**. Click the option to "**Link New Service.**" Select the music service you want to add.
- When you're connected to the music service of your choice, you can ask Alexa to

play music "Alexa, play Alicia Keys" or select your Echo device inside a music app and have it play there. If you want to play music on your Echo device from a selected music app let's say "**Pandora**," follow the steps below;

- To add Pandora to your Echo device, tap it on the "**Link New Service**" tab. At the Pandora skills page, and then tap the "**Enable to Use**" button.
- Input your Pandora account details, and grant Alexa permission to access your Pandora account. When your account is set up on the device, you will come back to the Pandora skill page; you'll be notified that the service has been successfully connected. Click "**Done**," and you can begin listening to music undeterred.
- Keep including some other services you wish to utilize. After you're done, you can set a particular service as the default. You should see all the new services you have recently added from the bottom of the Alexa app.
- Choose **Default Services** and select the service you wish to set as the default.
- At this time, ask Alexa to play a song or album from the services you included. Typically, you should state the name of the service you want Alexa to play from, however setting the specific music service as the default makes that redundant.

- For instance, you would have to say, "Alexa, play Grenade by Bruno Mars from Spotify." However, setting a particular service as the default implies Alexa will play music from that service without you necessarily having to call out the service name.

Stream Playlist with Alexa Voice Command

- Turn the Bluetooth for your smartphone and position yourself with your phone near your Echo device and say, *"Alexa, pair."* Your Echo device goes into pairing mode
- Open the Bluetooth settings page on your smartphone. Wait for your Echo device to popup in the list of devices with which to pair. After it appears, tap on the name of your Echo device
- Your mobile phone or tablet should then pair with and connect to your Echo device. You'll see your Echo device listed as connected. Alexa also notifies you of the connection.

Stream Music via Bluetooth

- To pair your Echo and mobile device, make sure both gadgets are close to each other and then say, "Alexa, pair." Your Echo will, at that point, go into pairing mode. Open the Bluetooth settings screen on your mobile device and wait for your Echo to appear on the lists of available devices recognized by Bluetooth. Once your Echo appears, tap the name to connect. However, when the connection between both devices is successful, Alexa will inform you of the connection.

- To manually pair your mobile device and Echo, go to the Alexa app, tap **Devices > Echo and Alexa**, at that point select the Echo device you need to pair with your mobile device.
- In the Connected Devices area, tap the path to **Pair Alexa Gadget**. At that point, open the Bluetooth settings screen on your mobile device and tap the name of your Echo. Your Echo will, at that point, connect. Once this has been done, when you open a music app on your mobile, you can have it play through your Echo device.
- To disable your Echo Show from your mobile device, say, "Alexa, disconnect from [name of device]." Alexa reacts, "Now disconnected from [name of device]."
- You can likewise disable through the Alexa app. Open the screen for your Echo device and tap the section for Bluetooth Devices. Click the down arrow close to the name of your device and select **Disconnect**.

Listen to Podcasts on Amazon Echo

Listening to podcasts on your Amazon smart speaker is very easy and follows almost the same method as streaming music from different music services. In this section of the book, we'll explore how to listen and enjoy podcasts on your smart speaker.

Listen to Podcast without Adding Skills.

By default, Alexa podcasts about TuneIn. If you ask, "Alexa, play the podcast links, right, and center," the last episode of the service is called.

TuneIn even offers Amazon Prime users a premium subscription of $ 9.99 a month for $ 2.99 a month. In addition, non-Prime Alexa users can subscribe to $ 3.99 per month.

While you cannot name a particular episode of a podcast, you can play the one that precedes the episode that is currently playing: "Alexa, play the previous episode."

If you temporarily switch to another podcast, music source, or other audio sources, Alexa will not be able to continue from its breakpoint. You have to restart the episode from the beginning.

You can also ask Alexa to just "play a podcast," and she'll play one she does not like, inevitably. (The niche nature of podcasts makes them so fantastic. Look for podcasts that suit your individual interests.)

Play Podcasts from the Alexa App

You can also use the Alexa application to find and control podcasts.

- Open the Alexa app on your mobile device.
- From the main menu, select **Music, Video, and Books**.
- Under **Music**, select **TuneIn**.
- Choose Podcasts
- You can also use the TuneIn search bar at any time to find a particular podcast.
- Browse categories to discover a podcast of interest and then a specific episode.
- At the top of the application, select the speakers you want.
- Click on the cover of the podcast to play it.

Play Podcasts in Alexa with a Routine

A routine is like a shortcut to let Alexa know what to do. It can be based on a command or a time of day.

- Open the Alexa app.
- Tap the **Menu** icon in the upper left corner.
- Tap on Routines.
- Touch the blue **plus sign** (+).
- Select the event Alexa should respond to. In this case, use voice.
- Enter the expression you want to use. Example: "Play my favorite podcast." Touch **Save**
- Tap the action + **add** sign.
- Touch **Select Music Provider**, and then select **TuneIn**.
- **Enter** the name of your podcast, and then tap Add.
- Review your selection and then touch **Add** again.
- Touch **Create**. Now you can tell your Echo device to play your podcast.

Podcast Playback in Alexa with AnyPod

The TuneIn ability in Alexa is still a bit awkward. Enable the AnyPod feature for a more seamless podcast listening experience. To do this on your echo device, simply say, "**Alexa, enable the AnyPod ability**." Or, follow these steps by running the app on your phone:

- Open the Alexa app.
- Tap the **Menu** icon in the upper left corner.
- Touch **Skills** in the menu.
- Enter "**AnyPod**" in the search bar and touch the search icon.
- In the search list, tap **AnyPod**.
- On the AnyPod screen, tap **Activate**.
- Now you can play AnyPod on your echo device with a voice command like "Alexa, please play AnyPod."

Additional commands to control Alexa are:

"Alexa, ask AnyPod," What are my subscriptions?"

"Alexa, ask AnyPod to rewind for five minutes."

"Alexa, play the next episode [or the previous one]."

Want to know more about AnyPod? Open the main menu of the Alexa application and go to **Skills> Your skills> AnyPod**. Here you can find information about AnyPod Skill and a link that gives you access to the entire user guide.

Stream Podcast via Bluetooth

Make sure your device is disconnected from existing Bluetooth connections.

- Set your smartphone or tablet in Bluetooth pairing mode.
- Switch your Echo device to pairing mode.
- On your phone or tablet, select your echo speaker in the Bluetooth Settings screen.
- Alexa tells you when to connect.

Listen to Audiobooks

To enable your Echo Show as your reading kit can be fascinating. To view books that can be read by Alexa, the following steps will be helpful.

- Launch the Alexa app
- Click on the **Menu** button on the upper left corner of the screen
- Select "**Music, Video, & Books**."
- Slide to the "**Books**" segment and select the option for Kindle. The app will then

display a rundown of all the ebooks Alexa can read.

- Tap on the name of a book to incite Alexa to begin the readout. On the other hand, you can say: "Alexa, read [title of the book.]" and the voice assistant will inadvertently authenticate your command.
- After Alexa commences, you can control the reading process (pause, play, rewind, forward, etc.) through your voice. To control it through the app, tap on the Volume symbol at the bottom right of the screen.
- In case you're an Audible subscriber from the Alexa app, tap on the "**Menu**" icon and select "**Music, Video & Books**." Swipe down to the segment for Books and tap on the option for **Audible**. Follow the same steps as you did for the Kindle to control Alexa.

Listen to the Radio with Alexa

- Open the Alexa app.
- Click on the Menu icon
- Choose **Skills & Games**.
- Look for the skill you want, or click on Categories, then select either Music & Audio or News to browse stations and skills.

- Choose the skill you want
- Next, tap **Enable Skill**.
- Alternatively, just say, "Alexa, open skills," and tell the voice assistant the skill you want to enable.
- If Alexa shows a numerical list of options, reply with a number to confirm your selection.
- Alexa can play your favorite local station without enabling any skills; just say, "Alexa, play [station]." However, you can request stations by frequency, name, or call out the letters. Also, you can request specific old-time radio shows by name like "Vintage Radio."

CHAPTER 5- Video and Skype

Watch Youtube and Netflix Videos

While getting an Echo Show, it's impossible to rule out the possibility of streaming videos with it, how about using one of the biggest video streaming services and how best do you get to stream it lives on your Echo device? The steps below will be of great help.

- From your Echo Show, go to **Settings**
- Scroll to "**Legal and Compliance**"
- Tap "**Amazon.com Privacy Notice.**"
- Next, tap on "**Your Account,**" and you'll be redirected to Amazon Store
- Search for "**Google**" using Amazon search box
- Locate Search.Google.com and click on it
- Tap "**Google Privacy Policy Link.**"
- Tap the "**My Account**" tab on the top right, at that point, click on "**Search,**" or you can likewise straightforwardly tap on "**YouTube symbol.**"
- You can likewise scan for Netflix by following the same method.
- You'll have two different ways to watch YouTube on the Echo Show. The principal path is with Amazon's very own Silk program.

- All you will need to do is say, "Alexa, open Silk browser." The internet browser will load. Tap on the YouTube bookmark or type the web address on the search bar. You can log in to your YouTube account to get customized and recommended videos. Secondly, load Firefox by saying, "Alexa, open Firefox" and then proceed from there.

Watch Amazon Prime Video

You can easily stream videos using Amazon Prime Video on Echo Show. Echo devices can play videos accessible through your Prime Video Subscription and from Amazon Channels Subscription like Starz, HBO, and Showtime.

- To scan from Videos library, say "Alexa, Show me my Video Library" at that point ask "Alexa, Show me my Watch List."
- To locate a particular title, you can say, "Alexa, show me '[title].'" Or "Alexa, scan for [search for TV shows]." "Alexa, Show me [Actor] Movies." "Alexa, Show me [Genre]."

To know more commands for TV and other Video Services, you have to activate Alexa Video Skills in your Alexa App. To enable the skills, follow the steps below;

- Tap on Menu and click "**Settings.**"

- Select "**TV and Video** "
- Next, choose Video or TV Service, provider
- Next, tap **Enable Skill**
- You see some guidance on screen, follow the instructions to connect Alexa to your video-service effectively
- Finally, click on "**Finish Setup.**"
- When it gets connected, you will see your devices under the "**Listed Devices.**"
- From there, the setup will be completed. Alexa App will open a "**Setting**" screen for the Alexa Skill. Under setting part, select TV or Video Service under the "**TV & Video**" area. You can now use your voice to control your TV and Video services.

Skype on Echo Show

Microsoft has revealed that you can now make use of your Echo devices to make Skype calls.

- Open the Alexa app.
- Click on **Settings**
- Tap on **Communication**
- Click on **Skype**.
- Next, type in your Skype account details.
- Simply say "Alexa, Skype Josh," or "Alexa, call [number] on Skype." The person you're calling must have the newest version of Skype.

CHAPTER 6- Settings for Smart Home Devices

Set Up Smart Home Devices

Controlling the lightings, plugs, and switches in your home using Alexa can be amazing, and it takes a few minutes to set up. Here are the steps on how to do that.

- Launch your Alexa app and tap the **Menu** icon.
- Next, tap **Smart Home**

- Select **Add Device**.

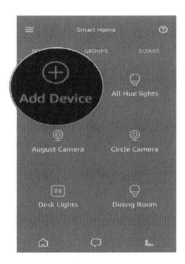

- From the menu, select the devices you want to install
- Choose the brand you're using. For instance, Leviton, Philips Hue, or GE. In case you're utilizing a brand other than Amazon, download the brand's app to complete the setup process and set up your device adhering to the brand's app guidelines.
- When you're done setting up the device, come back to the Amazon Alexa app and tap on **Skills & Games** from the menu option.
- Explore the brand you're using and tap "**Enable To Use**."
- Log in with your account details for that brand, so whatever you used to sign in to the brand's apps, this will connect to your Amazon Echo account.
- However, if you're using Amazon smart home devices, the steps are different. After

you've chosen Amazon as your smart home gadget brand, tap **Next** to wrap up setting up.

- Amazon will request your 2D barcode in the quick guide that accompanied your gadget. You can likewise check the back of your gadget to check whether it has a barcode. Tap **Scan Barcode** and complete the setup by following prompt.
- After setup is complete, you can now use Alexa to control the process by using the following phrases; "Alexa, turn on the kitchen light." "Alexa set kitchen light to 60%." "Alexa, turn off the AC in the room." "Alexa, turn off the room light."

Create Smart Home Groups

As you include an ever-increasing number of smart home gadgets that work with the Amazon Echo, it can get hard to recollect what you named every gadget. More terrible, when you need to control numerous gadgets in a solitary room, you need to state, "Alexa, do this. Alexa, do that. Alexa, accomplish something different." The uplifting news is, you can make smart home groups for Alexa that does everything from a single voice command. The steps to do this are listed below;

- Go to the Alexa app.

- Click on the **Devices** symbol in the bottom left corner.
- On the Devices page, tap the **plus** icon (+) in the top right corner.
- From the options that appear, tap **Add Group**.

- On the **Group Name** screen, type a name into the field or tap the **Custom Name** field and pick whatever name you like and then tap **Next** to continue.

- On the **Define Group** screen, select the Alexa-enabled device from which you need to trigger the command.
- If you pick just a single device, that will be the sole device from which you'll have the option to tell Alexa to control this specific smart homegroup. If you need to control the smart home group from any of the Alexa –enabled devices in your home, you should choose them all.
- At that point, slide to the **Devices** area of the **Define Group** page and pick the smart home devices you need to add to the group. For instance, if you need to control every one of the lights in the family room with a particular command, you would choose just those smart bulbs, switches, or plugs that control those lights.
- After you pick which smart home gadgets to add, tap **Save,** and the smart home group will be created, and you'll be redirected to the Devices page.

- When you have made the smart homegroup, you can inform Alexa to turn on or off that group. Alternatively, you can do this via the Alexa app.

Editing a Smart Home Group

If you purchase a brand new Echo device, and you want to add it to your smart home group, or you want to remove a particular device or delete a smart homegroup, then this is the right piece for you.

- Launch the Alexa app from your phone.
- Tap the **Devices** symbol in the bottom left corner.
- On the "**Device Group**" page, tap Edit in the top right corner.
- On the "**Edit Group**" page, select or deselect the Echo devices you need to control the group and the smart home devices you need to add to the group.
- Click on the **Save** button, and the new smart home device will be added to the group.

Delete a Smart Home Group

- Launch the Alexa app.
- Click the Devices icon in the bottom left corner.
- While on the Devices screen, tap the group you need to delete.
- Next, tap **Edit** in the top right corner.
- On the "**Edit Group**" page, select the delete icon in the top right corner.
- You'll be prompted to confirm the deletion. Tap **Delete** to confirm. After which a confirmation message will appear at the top of the screen.

Set Up and Control Smart Thermostats

If you're using a smart thermostat for your home and you want to control the smart thermostat with Alexa voice prompt, this is quite an impressive feature because you can increase or reduce the degree without touching the device. for this guide, I'll use the Ecobee3, but all other smart home devices or thermostat follows the same step

To connect your Ecobee3 to your Amazon Echo, follow the steps below:

- Launch the Alexa app on your smartphone

- Tap the Menu icon and select **Smart Home** from the list
- Scroll down until you see Get More Smart Home Skills, then tap on the arrow
- Next, type "**Ecobee**" in the search box and tap the first result with the Ecobee logo
- Tap **Enable Skill**
- Log in to your Ecobee account
- Select **Accept**
- When your Amazon Echo and Ecobee3 Thermostat have been connected, there are a few commands you can say. The main thing you need to remember is the name of your thermostat, as assigned by the Ecobee app. If you don't give the particular name, Alexa will request that you confirm the name you have assigned to the thermostat. You can:
- Set temperature by saying, "Alexa, set (thermostat name) to 50." Use Alexa to customize it further the way you want.

CHAPTER 7- Intercom and Privacy

Setup Alexa's Drop-In

To start utilizing Echo Drop-In as an intercom, you should sign up for Alexa Calling and Messaging on the Alexa app and then activate Drop In on your device. Just follow the steps below;

- Launch the Alexa app on your smartphone.
- Tap the **Conversations** icon, the small text bubble icon at the bottom of the display.
- Follow the prompts to confirm your name and grant access to your contact list, then confirm your phone number (with an SMS code).
- Next, tap the **Menu** icon in the top left corner
- Tap **Settings** and choose the first Echo you wish to enable from the options.
- Under **General**, search for Drop-In and choose "**On.**"
- Tap **Drop-In** and select **Only My Household** to limit these features to only the devices in your home and then do the same for the rest of the devices (if you have more than one Echo device).
- If you have different Echo devices in your home, you will need to give name each one

58

uniquely; this enables you to use the intercom feature effectively.

- Launch the Alexa app and then click on the "**Menu**" icon at the upper left side of the display.
- Tap **Settings** and tap the Echo you need to name.
- Click **Edit Name**.
- Erase the present name and enter another one. Do this for the rest of your devices.
- Once the above step is completed, you can say "Alexa, drop in on the Sitting Room" to any of the other Echo devices in your home; this will automatically connect, and you'll be able to communicate with anybody in the sitting room.
- If you are utilizing an Echo Show, you will see a **Recently Active** marker showing whether somebody is close to the rest of the Echo devices in your home.
- You can also use this feature to broadcast other announcements to other rooms while sitting in the comfy of your room.

Drop-In on Friends and Family

Having contacts on your device phonebooks approves you for Drop-In, you can say, "Alexa, Drop-In on [contact name]." Just make sure the name appears as it is in your address book. If you want to turn it off, say, "*Alexa, video off,*" or touch the screen and select it that way.

Also worth noting: if you don't want people Dropping In on you say, "Alexa, don't disturb me," and that will do the trick.

Extend Drop-In beyond your Household.

To Drop In on, and receive Drop-Ins from, devices not within your household, you'll have to apply the necessary permission for each device's contact:

- Tap the **Conversations** icon on the home screen of the Alexa app.
- Next, click the **Contacts** icon at the upper-right corner.
- Select the contact.
- Finally, toggle **Allow Drop-In**.
- The contact will have to grant you the same permission.

View approved Drop-In contacts

- Tap the **Conversations** icon on the home screen of the Alexa app.
- Click the **Contacts** icon at the top-right.
- Select yourself.
- You can now view your approved contacts beneath the "**People Who Can Drop-In.**"

- You can also view and edit the Drop-In permissions of individual contact by choosing them one after the other.

Delete Alexa History via Alexa App

Erasing Alexa recordings is an essential piece of your privacy. However, you should know that Alexa utilizes your recordings to help improve the accuracy of its listening and help optimize your experience and use of the device. The more you converse with Alexa, the more brilliant it moves toward understanding your voice. So, when you delete all your recordings, you're disposing of Alexa's "*memory*" of your voice, so Alexa may experience more difficulty understanding your directions.

Did you know Alexa records all that you say? Alexa devices, for instance, store recordings of your history of directions or Alexa-related dialog, this information is stored in the Amazon Cloud. If you're privy about your privacy and wants to delete all your Alexa conversations and logged in commands, you can easily do that with the steps below:

- Launch the Alexa app from your smartphone

61

- From the Alexa app home screen, tap the **Menu icon** and select **Settings**
- From the display options, select **Alexa Account.**

- At the bottom of the display screen, tap **Alexa Privacy** to begin
- Next, select **Review Voice History** from the displaying options; this will open another screen with all your recorded Alexa conversations.

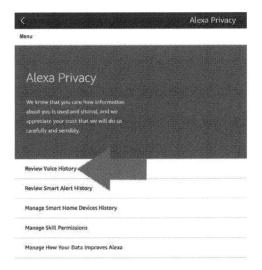

- Select the range of dates to view your conversations by date, or you can filter out all your recordings by tapping **All History**; this will show all your conversations with Alexa when they happened, and on what device
- To removing conversations, select the checkbox of each conversation that you need to delete. At that point, tap **Delete Selected Recordings** to remove
- To delete everything is simple, go back to the **Review Voice History** menu and select **Delete All Recordings for All History** to complete.

Delete Alexa History via PC

You can likewise delete your conversation history from your PC, to do this follow the instructions below.

- Login to www.amazon.com/mycd and enter your login details; this will direct you to the **Manage Your Content and Devices** page
- Ensure you are in the **Devices** tab. Here you will see all the devices associated with your Amazon account. Select your Amazon Echo device; underneath the name of the device, you'll see an option that says **Delete Voice Recordings**; Select this, and Amazon will display a disclaimer screen.
- From the popup screen, select **Delete**, you should receive a message that says *Your deletion request was received*!

Set Up Parental Controls

Follow the steps below to enable FreeTime on your Echo device:

- Open the Alexa app on your smartphone

- Tap the Menu icon at the top left corner of the screen and from the displaying options, select **Alexa Devices**
- Select Amazon Echo from the list
- Scroll down, and then select **FreeTime** under **General**
- Toggle on the **FreeTime** button
- Next, select **Setup Amazon FreeTime**
- Type in your child's first name, select the child gender and enter the birthdate
- Select an icon and tap **Add Child**
- Tap **Continue**, then enter your Amazon password and tap "**Sign In**." you may be asked to make confirmations through two-factor authentication and follow prompt

Once this feature is enabled, you can turn on and off features you want to restrict or allow for your kids. To set further modifications, login to https://www.parents.amazon.com, where you can set **Daily Time Limits** and other functions.

Remove Explicit Music

If you don't want your kids to listen to some explicit content or view explicit content, you can set that up through the Alexa app on your smartphone by following the steps below:

- Launch the Alexa app

- Tap the **Menu icon** and select **Settings**
- Select **Music** under **Preferences**
- Tap **Explicit Filter** and turn on the button next to it.

CHAPTER 8- Phone Calls, Messaging, Alexa Wake Word & Accent

Set Up Alexa Calling and Messaging

It's no news that you can make phone calls with your Echo device, to do this you must first sign up for this feature after which you can either decide to manually make calls or use the Alexa voice command to contact anybody on your contact list as it appears on the Alexa app.

- Open the Amazon Alexa app
- Tap the **Communication** tab at the bottom of the display.
- On the **Commination** screen, tap on **Get Started.**
- Choose your name from the list that pops up and tap **Continue**.
- If prompted to grant Alexa permission to access your contacts, tap **Allow**.
- Follow the on-screen instructions to verify your phone details and complete the setup.

Send Text Message

- Just say, "Alexa, send a message."
- Alexa will reply with, "To whom?"
- Tell Alexa the name of the contact you would like to send a message to.
- When you've chosen the recipient, Alexa will ask, "What's the message?"
- Say out the message you want to send. When you're done speaking, Alexa will reckon, "Got it. Should I send it?"
- Reply with "Yes," and Alexa will automatically send the message to the contact you selected.

You can also send messages directly from the Alexa app by following the steps below:

- Tap on **Message** from the **Communication** page.
- Select a contact on the **Start Conversation** page.
- After you've chosen a contact, you'll be redirected to the messaging screen. You'll see three options at the top: Call, Video Call, and Drop-In.
- To send a text message, input the message into the Type your message text box at the lower part of the display. Alternatively,

tap the blue microphone icon to send a voice message.

- After you're finished, the microphone icon will change to an upward arrow. Click on the icon to send the message.
- The message will be delivered to the contact's Echo and to the Alexa app on their smartphone. If the contact does not have an Echo device, the message will be delivered to the text app on their phone.

Make Phone Calls

- Open the Alexa app
- Tap on the **Conversation** bubble icon at the bottom of the screen to go to the **Communications** section.
- Alexa will require you to verify your name and grant it permission to access your phone's contacts list (if you haven't set it up). You'll have to confirm your phone number. The process is very easy, and Alexa will guide you with on-screen directions.
- Abbreviated codes such as 311, numbers with letters are also prohibited. Also, you cannot call numbers outside the US. UK, Mexico, and Canada.
- It is worth noting that you can call an Echo device outside the US and UK.

However, it must be located in a country where Alexa calls to Alexa are supported.

- Once the setup is complete, you can make your first call. Just say "Alexa" or whatever you've set up as the wake-up word. Follow by "call [contact's name]." If you need to call your friend Josh, the command will be: "Alexa, call Josh." Alexa will then call him.
- If Josh has an Echo device with enabled calls, Alexa will ring his Echo device. If he does not have an Echo device or it does not have enabled calls, Alexa will then make contact with Alexa on Josh's phone. Similar to Echo devices, Alexa, on his phone, will need to have enabled calls.
- If Josh doesn't have Alexa on his phone or the calls feature is not enabled, Alexa will proceed to dial the number you've specified in the Contacts. If there's more than one number associated with Josh, Alexa will prompt you to select which one you want to dial. Choose the number, and Alexa then will dial it.
- To end the call, say, "Alexa, hang up."

If you've already set up your phone number, then the steps below will make it easier:

- Open the Alexa app from your mobile phone
- Tap the **Conversations** menu at the bottom of the screen

- Tap the Contacts icon to view your available Alexa-to-Alexa contacts.
- Select the contact you want to get across to and then select the phone icon (Call)
- To end the call, tap the **End** button onscreen.

How to Receive a Call

You can also receive calls from your contacts via your Echo. If a contact calls you, your Echo's light ring will go green, and Alexa will notify you that someone's calling you.

If case you've not given Alexa permission to your contacts list, you'll be alerted that an unknown number is calling you. To answer, just say, "Alexa, answer." To reject the call just say, "Alexa, ignore."

How to Block a Number

To block a number, it has to be in your Contacts; you can't block random numbers.

- Open the Alexa app.
- Go to the **Calling & Messaging** section.

- Tap on the Contacts icon; it is located in the upper right corner.
- Click on the three dots when the next screen displays.
- Next, click on **Block Contacts** and select the contact you wish to block.

How to Change Alexa Wake Word

- Open the Alexa app and tap on the **Menu** bar on the left side
- Tap **Settings**.
- Select **Device Settings**.
- Choose your device from the list.

Alternatively,

- Touch **Devices** from the bottom of the Alexa app.
- Choose either **Echo & Alexa** or **All Devices.**
- Select your device from the list.
- Move down to the **General** section and click on **Wake Word**.
- Select a new word from the list. Aside from Alexa, you can choose the **Echo**, **Computer**, or **Amazon**.
- After choosing a new wake word, you'll notice a brief pop-up message telling you

to know it may take some minutes to make the change. Click on **OK**. Also, your Amazon Echo speaker will emit a light flash orange.

- So, that's it, your new Wake Word is set and ready for use.

How to Change Alexa's Accent

- Launch the Alexa app
- Tap the **Devices** icon on the bottom right corner of the menu
- Select the **Echo & Alexa** icon on the upper left
- Click on the device for which you intend to change Alexa's accent
- Move down and click on **Language** under the **General** section
- Next, click the accent/language of your choice to finish up.

Setup Do Not Disturb

You can likewise activate the Do Not Disturb feature to stop notifications for calls and messages, just as avert Drop-In contact on a particular device. To turn on Do Not Disturb, say,

"Alexa, turn on, do not disturb me." To turn off, say, "Alexa, turn off Do Not Disturb.

To manually turn off from the Alexa app follow the steps below;

- From your phone, launch the Alexa app.
- Click on the **Menu** icon in the top left corner of the screen.
- Select **Alexa Devices**.
- Choose your device.
- Tap **Do Not Disturb** option and then click on **Enable Scheduled**.
- Tap **Start** and then click **End** to set the times.

CHAPTER 9- Alexa Shopping

Set Up Alexa for Shopping

I've always been concerned about keeping things as simple as possible; when it comes to stocking your shopping list, it's not as difficult as it may seem. However, two parameters are important; one is having Amazon Prime membership while the other is activating the 1-Click ordering option. You should know if you have a Prime membership, so let's talk about how to enable the 1-Click order option.

- Log in to the Amazon website and click on **Payment Options**.
- Next, tap 1-Click Settings and toggle on the switch if the feature is off. With this, you're good to proceed to the net stage.

So, how do you enable voice purchase for Alexa? Read the steps below to find out.

- Launch the Amazon Alexa app from your mobile device.
- Tap the **Menu** icon.
- Select **Settings**.
- Slide down and tap **Voice Purchasing**.
- Under **Purchase by Voice**, toggle the slider to enable the feature.
- To prevent the unauthorized purchase, you should create a code (PIN). Under the

Voice Code option, utilize the slider to enable the feature.

- Tap the box by the side of **Voice Code** to choose a PIN and click **Save**.
- When you're prepared to make a purchase with the voice assistant, just say, "Alexa, order a laptop." Alexa will display an array of options on the screen of your Echo Show; from there you can make your decision, and if you fancy any item tap "**Purchase This**" option.
- If Alexa inquires as to whether you're prepared to make the purchase, reply with "**Yes**." The product will be placed in your Amazon cart, and if you've set up a PIN, you'll be asked to say out the pin before the order can be processed through Amazon checkout. If you request something accidentally, you have 30 minutes to cancel the order.

Manage Alexa Voice Shopping

You can ask Alexa to order the items you need and get recommendations. Alexa will suggest Amazon Choice items, which are selected by user rating and price and are available for shipping.

Not only can you order, but you can also cancel the order. To order say "Alexa, add baby diaper to my cart" will add the item ready for you to complete the purchase online. But Amazon Prime users with one-click ordering turned on and have items bought straight away. To revoke or retract order, use the command "Alexa, cancel that order" will remove what you just ordered from your cart.

Do you care to get notification from Alexa when your purchased items are delivered? then follow the next tip.

Get Delivery Notifications

- Launch the Alexa app and then, tap the **Menu icon**
- From the displaying options, select **Settings**
- From the **Accounts** section, tap **Notifications**
- Select **Shopping Notifications**
- From the **Delivery Notifications** section, chose "**Out for delivery**" or "**Delivered.**"

Check Delivery Status

If you're wondering when an item is due to arrive, you can ask Alexa this as well.

When you ask, "Alexa, where's my stuff?" Alexa will provide information on when your next package will arrive. For a piece of detailed information about the items in your order, go to the Alexa app, and the home page will show your recent voice request with a link to "**View order details**."

Set Up Password for Voice Purchase

If you're scared someone or your kids might order products you didn't bargain for, then you can set up a password for your voice purchases by following the steps below:

- Launch the Alexa app
- Tap the **Menu icon**
- Next, tap **Alexa Account**
- Select Voice Purchasing and toggle on **Voice Code** and set a four-digit voice code. When you order via Alexa, you'll need to say the code to enable deductions from your payment settings and your item delivered.

Delete Alexa's Recordings

- To erase your Alexa voice recordings, launch the Alexa app.
- Tap **Settings**
- Select **Alexa Privacy**

- Click on **Review Voice History**. From here, you'll see a rundown of all your voice recordings since setting up your Echo device. Select the recordings you want to erase; you can choose to erase all recordings in entirety by choosing "**All History**" to delete all or if you prefer to erase all the recordings for a particular day let's say for today, tap on "**Delete All Recordings for Today**."

CHAPTER 10- Alexa Skills and Settings

Connect IFTTT with Alexa

IFTTT (If This Then That) is a smart technique for having every one of the bits of innovation in your home converse with each other. Since your smart speaker will converse with your lightings, it may not get along with that recently fitted smart smoke alert. You can make your very own customized commands using your Echo device. Connecting the IFTTT with Alexa can be done by following the steps below;

- Go to the IFTTT Alexa channel page on ifttt.com/amazon_alexa and click "**Connect**." On the other hand, look for Alexa in the IFTTT app.
- Sign in to your account or create one if you don't have an account already.
- You'll, at that point be prompted to sign in to your Amazon account to connect the two. Ensure you're using the exact account that is linked to your Echo devices.
- Now Amazon may request that you verify your account via email or SMS.
- Grant IFTTT permission to connect when prompted.
- Presently you can begin to nimble about what the applets have to offer. To enable an applet, select and tap the "**On**" toggle,

however, some might give you the option to customize.

Create New IFTTT

- Login to the IFTTT website and sign in
- Next, tap New Applet
- Click on "**+ this**" (i.e., the trigger)
- Search for "**Amazon Alexa**."
- Provide your Amazon account credentials.
- Select a trigger from the provided list
- Click on "**+ that**" (i.e., the action) and search for the action service you want to use, and then click on the icon
- Next, choose a specific action
- That's it; your Alexa trigger is set to cause an action on the particular service you selected. Have fun!

Setup Alexa Recipes Skills

Alexa can cook! That's massive if you ask me. Maybe you're prepping a meal, and it happens you've forgotten the instructions to prep the recipes and its ingredients, don't worry, Alexa can be your kitchen assistant. First, you have to enable this feature by following the steps below;

- Launch the Amazon Alexa App from your mobile device.

- Tap the **Menu** icon select **Skills**
- Search for "**Allrecipes**"
- Next tap the "**Enable**" option
- Next, link the "**Allrecipes**" account through Facebook.
- When the skills have been activated, ask Alexa to scan for your preferred recipes and save it from Allrecipe's official site.

You can use commands such as the following to trigger Alexa.

- "Alexa, open the Allrecipes Skill."
- "Alexa, find [name of recipe]."

If Alexa finds the recipes, you can use your voice command ["Alexa, begin cooking"] to play and pause the directions or by looking at the screen of your device. If you prefer the recipes sent to your phone, say, "Alexa, send the recipe to my phone."

Set Up Reminders

You can set this up either manually from the Alexa app or through voice command. So, let's start from the voice command.

- Simply say, "Alexa, create a reminder," the voice assistant will then ask you what the reminder is for.
- Disclose to Alexa what it is, for example, "visit Jude" "go get the kids from school."

Alexa then asks for the date and time. You can use either of this tag; "October, 21 at 05 pm," or "today at 3 pm," respectively.

- To set up a reminder manually, launch the Alexa app from your phone and tap on the **Menu** icon. Select the option for **Reminders and Alarms**. If there is more than one Echo device in your home, click on your preferred Echo from which you want to hear the reminder. From the Reminders area, tap **Add Reminder**.
- Fill in the appropriate fields; the date, the time, and the Echo device on which you need to hear the reminder. Tap **Save** to complete.
- You can check your reminders whenever by asking the voice assistant: "Alexa, what are my reminders?" and Alexa will read them to you. You can likewise view your reminders from the Reminders segment in the Alexa app.
- To delete a reminder, say, "Alexa, delete [name of reminder]" or all reminders by saying: "Alexa, delete all reminders."

Set Up Alarms

You can set an alarm for a particular day and time. Just say, "Alexa, set alarm." Alexa will then ask you to provide the day and time, follow prompt to save. However, you can say it in a more direct way,

"Alexa, set alarm for 05:00 pm today" or "Alexa, set alarm for 06 am tomorrow."

You can request a repetitive alarm to sound off each day by saying, "Alexa, set a repetitive alarm for 06 am every Saturday."

You can monitor your alarms by asking: "Alexa, what are my alarms?" Check the Alarms segment in the Alexa app to view your current alarms, or make new ones. Tap a particular alarm to adjust the time, change its sound, or erase it. Alternatively, you can say, "Alexa, erase [time of alarm]" or remove all alarms by saying: "Alexa, delete all alarms."

Set a Timer

You can easily create a timer for anything; maybe you're meditating intermittently for 5 minutes, you can ask Alexa to set a timer, so the time limit doesn't elapse without you knowing. You can say, "Alexa, set meditation timer for 5 minutes," when this time elapses, Alexa will trigger you from your Echo Show device.

Set To-Do Lists

You can add an item to your to-do list by telling Alexa straightforwardly by saying, "Alexa, add purchasing of the earpiece to my to-do list."

However, you can also do this from the Alexa app by tapping on the **Menu** icon and then tap the option for **Lists**. Swipe the thing to one side to check it as finished, then follow prompt to finish up.

Set Up and Receive Weather Report

With the Alexa weather report, you can request tomorrow's weather, the end of the week forecast, or for weather reports about any place.

To effectively get an accurate weather forecast, you can install one of the weather skills from the Alexa app. For this guide, I'll use the Big Sky Skill for illustration purposes. It will let you know precisely when downpour will occur and likely to stop.

To enable the Big Sky skill to follow the steps below:

- Open the Alexa app on your smartphone
- Tap the **Menu icon** and select **Skills**
- Search for Big Sky and tap **Enable Skill**
- To create a Big Sky account, click **Create One** at the bottom of the screen
- Enter a username and password to sign up

- Once signed in, enter the location for which you need to use for weather forecasts
- Select if you need basic or comprehensive forecast data
- Select Celsius or Fahrenheit and tap Submit to wrap up
- To trigger weather reports, call up Big Sky by using the Alexa voice command prompt, say, "Alexa, open Big Sky;" this will automatically give you the forecast for your chosen location. The Skill can tell you high and low temperatures and many more depending on your customization.
- There are various ways you can trigger the Big Sky skill to give you a weather report. "Alexa, ask Big Sky for the weather in 7 hours."

Set Up and Get Traffic Reports

From the Alexa app on your smartphone, you can include a location where you want to get traffic reports, and from that point, you can ask Alexa what traffic on your area is like, and Alexa will respond with a status of traffic in the area. Follow the steps below to add a destination for a traffic update.

- Open the Alexa app on your phone
- Tap the **Menu icon**

- From the displaying options, tap **Settings**
- Next, tap **Traffic**
- Tap **add address**
- Enter the address of your destination, and then tap **Save Changes**
- To trigger, use Alexa voice prompt to get live traffic updates.

Sync your Calendar with Alexa

Life can get occupied, and regardless of whether your calendar is on your smartphone in your pocket, it very well may be anything but difficult to overlook when you have an arrangement. Alexa is here to help, however, and can tell you when you have something coming up in your day. Anyway, before you can ask her what's on the books, you'll have to match up your calendar; this is a genuinely basic procedure; when you recognize what you're doing and shouldn't take more than a couple of minutes. Alexa can match up with calendars from Google, Microsoft, and even Apple; this implies notwithstanding when your schedule is on an alternate administration, Alexa can at present synchronize, so you never think twice. If you have diverse occasions on various records, at that point despite everything, you're free, since you can include different calendars, and even pick which occasions to disregard from inside the Alexa app.

- Open the Alexa app on your phone
- Tap the **Menu icon** (3-dash lines) in the upper left corner of the screen
- Tap **Settings**
- Scroll down and tap **Calendar**
- Tap the account type you want to sync with Alexa
- Tap **Link your calendar account**
- Tap the **allow** button in the lower right corner to complete.

Flash Briefings

Are there sure news, traffic and weather reports, or other essential information you want to hear every day automatically? If yes, then "Flash Briefings" is the answer. With this feature, you get reports and information about selected skills every day; this includes news from your favorite TV Channels. So, how do you set this up? The processes below will answer that.

- To add skills to your flash briefing, launch the Alexa app from your mobile device. At the Home screen, look for the "**Flash Briefing**" Alexa delivered to your device.

- Next, click on the "**More**" link, and after that, click on the link to customize your Flash Briefing.
- Alternatively, tap the **Settings** icon and choose "**Flash Briefing**." While on the Flash Briefing screen, you can deactivate or activate various skills if more than one is listed. To include more skills, tap on the option to "**Get more Flash Briefing content**."
- Alexa now takes you to a page showing skills you can add to your Flash Briefing. You can peruse every one of the skills or search for a particular skill by inputting a keyword followed by the world words "flash briefing."
- Click on the skill you wish to add and then tap the **Enable** button. You would then be able to return to the lists of skills, peruse for other skills that might tickle your fancy, and then enable the skill to add it to your Flash Briefing.
- When you're done adding skills, click on the Back button to come back to the Flash Briefing Settings layout. Cross-examine every skill you've added and choose which ones to retain and which to deactivate. The active skills will appear at the top of the screen in the "**On**" part, while the inactive ones appear at the base in the "**Off**" section.
- You can also arrange the skills in the sequence you want to hear them, to do this,

tap on the link to "**Edit Order**." Press and hold Menu icon close to the skill you want to move and then drag and drop into the ideal position and then click "**Done**."

- From here, you can now alert Alexa to play your Flash Briefing by saying, "Alexa, what's my Flash Briefing?" Alexa will then start from the first briefing on the list. If you want to go to the later briefing, say, "Alexa, next" and Alexa will execute your command.

CHAPTER 11- Alexa Commands, Questions and Easter Eggs

In this section, you will know what kind of questions you can ask your smart speaker in case they just gave you one and want to try to squeeze it to the fullest. They are all kinds of commands, from the most basic and essential to some more advanced ones, including other ways to ask the same thing and the occasional Easter egg.

News and Time Information

We will start with a series of commands with which you will be able to keep yourself informed. With them, you will be able to ask your Amazon Echo for the news of the day, both general and sports, as well as weather information.

Alexa, good morning: It greets you good morning, and then it shows you all the information of your day that you have configured in the routine.

Alexa, what is the news of the day? : Launch the news summary, taking the media you have configured in the application.

Alexa, what do you put on TV tonight? : You can ask him about the programming of the television networks.

Alexa, how was Madrid? : He will tell you the latest results of the team you tell him, as well as the next games you have.

Alexa, what is the league ranking? : It tells you the ranking of the league's team or some other sports competitions.

Alexa, what is the weather like? : It tells you the temperature and the weather in your city, and the forecast for the rest of the day.

Alexa, what is the weather like in Madrid? : It tells you the temperature and the weather in the city that you tell it, and the forecast for the rest of the day.

Alexa, is it going to rain this weekend? : You can ask if it's going to rain or it's going to be sunny, and he will tell you the answer related to your city.

Alexa, is it going to rain this weekend in Barcelona? : You can ask if it's going to rain or it's going to be sunny in a specific city, and it will tell you the answer.

Alexa, what is the weather going to be like in France? : When you ask about the weather in a country, it will ask you to specify the city, and when you answer it, it will tell you.

Alexa, what time is it? : Tells you the time.

Alexa, what time is it in Chicago? : It tells you what time it is in the city that you tell.

Alarms, Reminders, and Calendars

If your mind could use a little help to remind you of everything you should, Alexa has alarm systems, reminders, and calendars that can help you out. And these are precisely the commands that we are going to teach you in this next section. Yes, for having even has a way to postpone an alarm five more minutes in the morning

Alexa set an alarm: You start the process of setting the alarm, and Alexa will ask you the time.

Alexa, set an alarm for 7 in the morning: It will set an alarm for the next day at the time you tell it. If it is an alarm in the morning, it will ask if you also want to set it for the rest of the weekdays.

Alexa, wake me up at 8 in the morning with music: You will set the alarm with music, if you are listening to something it will configure you with music by that artist, using the music service that you have set by default.

Alexa, wake me up at 8 in the morning with Queen Music: You will set the alarm with the music of the artist you specify, using the music service you have set by default.

Alexa, cancel all my alarms: Cancel all alarms you have set.

Alexa, what alarms do I have? : It tells you the alarms you have set.

Alexa, postpone: You can also postpone alarms to sleep those five minutes more than they feel so good.

Alexa, set a reminder: Start setting a reminder. He will ask you first what the reminder is for, and then he will ask you when you want to remember it.

Alexa, remind me to take out the garbage at 9 o'clock at night: Set a reminder telling you all the information. You can also do it without specifying the time or topic to remember, and Alexa will ask you.

Alexa, tell me my reminders: It will tell you your next reminders.

Alexa, delete reminder: It will delete the reminder you have or ask you which one you want to delete.

Alexa, set a 5-minute timer: Alexa sets a timer, and it will notify you when the time you requested has elapsed.

Alexa, put a 10-minute pizza timer: In addition to creating them, you can also name the timers to distinguish them in case you use several.

Alexa, add "dinner with friends" to my calendar: Add the term "dinner with friends" to the calendar, and ask what time and at what time.

Alexa, add an event to my calendar: You start the entire process to add an event to the calendar, and it will ask you the name of the event, the day and the time.

Create and Manage your Lists

The shopping list, the to-do list, or even the ingredients you need to make that dish you like so much. Alexa allows you to create and manage your lists directly from the Amazon Echo without having to resort to the application, although all are synchronized with them to be able to consult them from your mobile.

Alexa, add tomatoes to my shopping list: Add the term tomatoes or whatever you say to the shopping list, one that comes pre-configured in Alexa.

Alexa, add watering the plants to my to-do list: Add the term water the plants or whatever you say to the to-do list, one of which is preconfigured in Alexa.

Alexa, create a list: You start the process of creating a list, and you will be asked the name and what you want to add.

Alexa, create a list with the name XXXX: By changing XXXX for any term, you will create a list with the name you want.

Alexa, add things to the XXXX list: Changing XXXX to the name of one of your lists, you start the process of adding something to that list. Alexa will ask you what you want to add.

Alexa, add [Item] to the XXXX list: By changing XXXX to the name of one of your lists, you add the item you said to that particular list.

Alexa, lists: The assistant will tell you which lists you have created.

Alexa, what do I have on my shopping list? : It tells you the items saved in the shopping list, or that it is empty if you have nothing.

Alexa, what do I have on my to-do list? : It tells you the items saved in the task list, or that it is empty if you have nothing.

Alexa, which is in the XXXX list: Changing XXXX to the name of a list you have created, the assistant will tell you what is inside.

Shopping with Alexa

Alexa and Amazon Echo are products of Amazon, one of the largest online stores in the world. Therefore, it is logical that they include commands that help you make purchases from the speaker without even having to open your computer or mobile. Be careful, because when you buy from Alexa everything can happen very fast and you can end up buying things without wanting to.

Alexa, I want to buy: He will ask you what you are looking for, and he will tell you the results of the term you tell him.

Alexa, I need to buy water: It will tell you the first two results that appear on Amazon with the term you have said.

Alexa, I want to buy technology: Alexa can also look for product types.

Alexa, buy the iPhone 11: If you tell him a specific product, Alexa will look for it so you can buy it.

Alexa, how is my shopping: It tells you what products you have added to your shopping cart.

Alexa, how is my purchase going: It will tell you when the orders you have placed on Amazon arrive, both from your Echo and from the web.

Music and Audio

Your Amazon Echo is still a speaker, smart or not, and that's why Alexa also has several commands with which to get the most out of this function. It offers you several controls with which to play music with different services, but also to listen to the radio, play ambient sounds, or even read books.

Alexa, play Beatles music: It will start playing random songs from the group you say on Amazon Music or Spotify, the service you have set by default.

Alexa, put Beatles music on Amazon Music: It will start playing random songs from the group that you say on Amazon Music or Spotify, the service you specify.

Alexa, put rock: If you have Amazon Music as a default service, it will put you on a rock music station or the genre you ask for. If you have Spotify, a playlist with a similar name will look for you.

Alexa, put party music: If you have Amazon Music as a default service, it will play you a party music station. If you have Spotify, a playlist with a similar name will look for you.

Alexa, put Queen: You can ask him for a specific artist, and he will offer you random songs.

Alexa, put the disk Disc Name: You can also ask for disc names, and it will look for them in the service you have preconfigured to play it.

Alexa, put 'Bohemian Rhapsody' by Queen: You can ask for specific songs to put on.

Alexa, put my Queen Playlist: It puts you a playlist that you have with the name you say, in this case, Queen.

Alexa, what song is this? : When you are listening to music, you can also ask for the exact song you are listening to.

Alexa, next: Go to the next song.

Alexa, previous: Go to the previous song.

Alexa, put Chain Dial: Put the radio station that you request in the service you have set to listen to the radio.

Alexa, give me the sound of a storm: If you need relaxing sounds like rain or a storm, Alexa can also play them.

Alexa, read the book 'American Gods': If you have the book purchased for Kindle, Alexa will read it with your robotic voice turning it into an audiobook.

General Information Questions and Calculations

Your Amazon Echo with Alexa can also act as an encyclopedia, dictionary, or calculator. Therefore, in this section, we are going to tell you some of the commands that you can use to ask general information questions, ask you to translate words or phrases and look for meanings. You can also do simple and compound mathematical calculations, as well as unit conversions.

Alexa, who is Cervantes? : You can ask Alexa to inform you about famous people, living or dead.

Alexa, how old is Penelope Cruz? : You can ask him about the age of celebrities, and in the answer, he will also tell you the date of birth.

Alexa, how do you say 'Thank you so much' in English: You can ask him to translate words into the language you want.

Alexa, when did man get to the moon? : You can ask him for the date on which historical events happened.

Alexa, how far is the moon? : It can tell you distances related to astronomy.

Alexa, how far is Galicia? : It also tells you the distance by car and straight line of your location, which depends on the zip code you have configured.

Alexa, how many inhabitants does Denmark have? : You can also ask him for various types of data about some countries, such as their population, information about the anthem or the flag.

Alexa, play the Danish anthem: You can ask him to make you play a hymn, and turn to Amazon Music or Spotify to do so.

Eastern Eggs

And we finish with the last section, in which we will include the rest of the commands that have been left out of the previous sections. This means that in this case, you will have a huge variety, with commands ranging from random content requests to others with games, jokes, or asking your assistant personal questions.

Alexa, what can you do? : It makes you a summary of things you can ask.

Alexa, surprise me: Perform random actions, such as playing small melodies.

Alexa, hello: Obviously, you can say hello to your assistant.

Alexa, why is your name Alexa?: It explains where the name comes from that Amazon decided to give the assistant.

Alexa, how old are you? : It tells you how old it is, or what is the same, the years it has been since the assistant was launched.

Alexa, tell me something: It tells you a curiosity about general knowledge.

Alexa, tell me something curious: Another command to get a curious anecdote about any topic of general knowledge.

Alexa, how are you? : He responds with his mood and then tells you a random curiosity.

Alexa, call XXXX: Replacing XXXX with the name of a contact on your mobile that also has an Amazon Echo.

Alexa, send a message to XXXX: Replacing the XXXX with the name of a contact on your mobile that also has an Amazon Echo.

Alexa, face, or cross? : It tells you face or crosses randomly.

Alexa, roll a dice: It tells you a number from one to six.

Alexa, tell me a number from one to one hundred: It tells you a random number between the amounts you tell it.

Alexa, rock, paper, or scissors: It tells you randomly rock, paper, or scissors.

Alexa, tell me a story: Start telling you a complete story.

Alexa, tell me the story of Little Red Riding Hood: He tells you a specific story that you ask.

Alexa, tell me a joke: He tells you a random joke.

Alexa, tell me some football: He tells you a football story.

Alexa, tell me a riddle: Alexa tells you a riddle.

Alexa, sing a song: Sing a random short song.

Alexa, sing a lullaby: Sing a random lullaby.

Alexa, what is your favorite color? : You can ask him for his favorite color.

Alexa, who is your favorite singer? : He tells you about singers, referring to details about some of his songs.

Alexa, what is your favorite game: It also responds ingeniously when you ask about its game, actor, and other things.

Alexa, where do you live? : He tells you he's here, but his head in the cloud.

Alexa, do you know how to rap? : You can ask Alexa to rap for you.

Alexa, tell me a movie phrase: It tells you a quote from a random movie.

Alexa, recommend me a Skill: He suggests you try some Skills.

Alexa, open [Skill Name]: Open and start using a Skill you have installed.

Alexa, let's play: Game Skills offers you.

Alexa, I want to meditate: It offers you a meditation skill.

Alexa, do me a magic trick: A funny magic trick.

Alexa, silver or lead: You can ask him questions related to movies.

Alexa, help me cook: Open a cooking skill and help you find a recipe.

Alexa, open my horoscope: Your daily horoscope is also available to your speaker.

Alexa, what do you want to talk about? : She has come to talk about her book.

CHAPTER 12- Troubleshooting

Your Echo device will most likely not last forever, and it's also likely to develop some issues due to some complicacy. However, I've outlined some common issues experienced while using my Echo device, too, and I hope these will help you.

Alexa Is Not Responding

If you say your device's wake word and Alexa does not respond, it is likely to be a couple of issues. To start with, ensure your device has power and internet connection.

- If there's a strong red light ring rather than a strong blue one, that means the microphone has been disabled. Press the microphone button at the top of your Echo to turn it on.
- If you have arrays of Alexa devices, the wrong one may hear and react to the wake word. Although Amazon uses Echo Spatial Perception to figure out which device is nearest to you, the false Echo may still respond.
- Check the Alexa app to ensure all devices are set up on one Amazon account.
- Separate the devices so that the one you need to respond to is nearer to where you are talking.

- However, if the wrong Echo still responds, you should change the wake word for one of the Echo devices.

Alexa Plays Music on the Wrong Device

Did you ask Alexa to play music in one room, and it starts playing in another room in an entirely different device? The issue emerges from how these Echo devices are grouped. Follow the steps below to rectify.

- Launch the Alexa app from your phone.
- Tap **Devices**.
- Choose the Group you wish to ungroup.
- Tap **Edit**.
- Finally, tap the **Delete** icon.
- When you've ungrouped the culpable devices, you can regroup them. The key is to guarantee that no default speaker is chosen. Else, you'll keep on having a similar issue.

Streaming Issues on Alexa Devices

- Switch off devices that are not in use but are connected to Wi-Fi.
- Draw the Echo nearer to the wireless router and put away from walls, metallic

items, or other possible causes of obstruction.

- Switch off the modem and router.
- Hold up 30 seconds.
- Restart the modem and the switch.
- Next, turn off the Alexa device and afterward turn it back on again.

Alexa Isn't Connected to Wi-Fi

Check the light on your Echo. If it is orange, the Wi-Fi connection isn't working appropriately, to fix this anomaly follow the hints below;

- Go to **Settings** and tap **Wi-Fi**.
- Input the network password and then turn off the modem and router.
- Wait for 30 seconds.
- Restart the modem and router
- Turn off your Echo and turn it back on again.
- Check updates for your router or modem firmware.

Issue with Alexa Intercom

- Check your contacts. If you added a new contact, Alexa probably has not included it yet.
- Exit and relaunch the Alexa app.

- Tap the **Conversations** tab and scan for the contact you are attempting to call.
- If the contact is already listed, ensure the phone number is correct.
- Sign out of the Alexa app and sign back in and if the issue is not still resolved, tap the Menu icon and click **Settings**, select **Sign Out** and then sign back in and try to make the call again.

Alexa Can't Find a Device

- Try setting up the device on your Wi-Fi network through the manufacturer's app.
- Log on to alexa.amazon.com and attempt to finish the setup from there. Deactivate and re-enable the skill for your smart home device in the Alexa app.
- From the Disable option in the Smart Home area of the Alexa app, disconnect the smart home device.
- Next, reactivate the smart home device once more.
- Check for updates for the device.
- Finally, say, "Alexa, find my devices," to enable Alexa to search for the smart home device once more.

Bluetooth Issues with Alexa

- Ensure the Bluetooth device is fully charged.
- Move the Bluetooth device as well as the Echo away from components of obstruction.
- Next, launch the Alexa app.
- Select **Alexa Devices** from the menu.
- Choose **Bluetooth Devices** and afterward tap **Clear**.
- Restart the smart home device and your Echo Show.
- Finally, pair your Alexa device and the Bluetooth device once more.

Reset Your Amazon Echo

If all troubleshooting has failed, the next thing in line is to reset your Echo device. You must note that when you reset your Echo device factory settings, you'll have to register it to your Amazon account again and customize other device settings.

- Press and hold the Reset button with a paper clip.
- Pause while the light ring on the device turns orange and afterward blue.
- Watch out for the light ring to switch off and afterward turn on again. At the point

when the light turns orange, the device will enter the setup mode.

- Finally, connect your Echo to the Wi-Fi network and register it to your Amazon account with the Alexa app.

CONCLUSION

Amazon Echo is an amazing device, I hope you find this guide useful and insightful, and it has helped you to find solutions to the most important features you ever wanted. Good luck and cheers.

ABOUT AUTHOR

Aaron Madison is a computer jerk, researcher, and a gadget perfectionist who loves to have all the latest gadgets. He loves to teach people how to use their devices and maximize its potential; He knows how to satisfy gadgets freaks and where to look to satisfy the teeming number of tech lovers. Aaron likes teaching the most complicated of things and making it simple for users. Aaron always gives you an "awe feeling." You have no option but to love him when he writes as he includes all the necessary details and information.

Made in the USA
Columbia, SC
04 December 2019